❖ 500 ❖
Great Things
About
Being a Dad

❖ 500 ❖ Great Things About Being a Dad

Steve Delsohn

**Andrews McMeel
Publishing**

Kansas City

01 02 03 04 05 RDC 10 9 8 7 6 5 4 3 2 1

ISBN: 0-7407-1530-5

Library of Congress Catalog Card Number: 00-108493

BOOK DESIGN AND COMPOSITION BY KELLY & COMPANY

For my father,
Norman Delsohn,
who taught me what
it means to be a dad

Acknowledgments

Above all, I want to thank my wife, Mary Kay, and our three daughters, Emma, Hannah, and Grace. They bless me with their love and tenderness.

For their various contributions, I'd also like to say thanks to David Black, Allan Stark, Patrick Dobson, Kelly Gilbert, Sheldon Gottlieb, David Rubenstein, Matt Gee, David Eisenstein, Rich Fish, Joe Smigiel, Aaron McKissich, Steve Duddy, and especially Phil McPherson.

⋇ 500 ⋇
Great Things
About
Being a Dad

❧ 1 ❧

Seeing your daughter
make her first contact
in T-ball . . . and
watching her run
to third base.

❧ 2 ❧

Seeing her graduate
from diapers to
"big girl" panties.

❧ 3 ❧

Every holiday feels
alive and fresh when you
experience it through
your child's eyes.

❧ 4 ❧

Eventually,
your children fall
asleep and you can
regain the remote control.

❖ 5 ❖

While they're awake,
you have an excuse
to watch *Rugrats.*

❖ 6 ❖

You have an excuse
to see all the new
kid movies at
the theater.

❖ 7 ❖

You can get
hugs and kisses
when you're sad.

❖ 8 ❖

The thrill of hearing
your child read
her first book.

❈ 9 ❈

Finally, you
feel like a man
instead of a guy.

❈ 10 ❈

Your kids still
love you when you
screw up at work.

❧ 11 ❧

Seeing your daughter's
team get blasted in
soccer . . . and then
hearing her say
she still had fun.

❧ 12 ❧

The strange feeling
of pride the first time
your kid beats you
in Monopoly.

❧ 13 ❧

You get to watch these
classic Disney movies:
*The Lion King, Robin Hood,
Beauty and the Beast,
The Aristocats, One Hundred
and One Dalmatians.*

❧ 14 ❧

You have something
to discuss (your kids)
when you meet strangers
who insist on conversation.

❖ 15 ❖

You get to throw
your back out
playing Twister.

❖ 16 ❖

Once your back is destroyed,
you can lie in bed like a slug,
watch ESPN for hours, and
demand that your children
keep bringing refreshments.

❖ 17 ❖

How incredibly shrewd
you feel when you figure
a way to make your
baby stop wailing.

❖ 18 ❖

Having your warm,
cuddly toddler climb
into bed with you
on Sunday morning.

❖ 19 ❖

Hearing
your toddler
ask for a piece
of "yicken."

❖ 20 ❖

Hearing
her ask if she
can sit on
your "yap."

❖ 21 ❖

Hearing
her tell people
she's still "yittle."

❖ 22 ❖

If Mommy goes to sleep
when the kids do, you can
call your best friend in Chicago
and gossip about the girls you
knew in high school.

❧ 23 ❧

Volunteering in your
child's class and seeing
her eyes light up
when you walk in.

❧ 24 ❧

Volunteering in her class
and hearing her answer
a question correctly
while you're there.

❧ 25 ❧

Returning
from a business trip
and getting tackled by
your rowdy children.

❧ 26 ❧

Returning
from a business
trip with presents
from faraway places.

❖ 27 ❖

You have a reason
to stock up on
double-cream Oreos.

❖ 28 ❖

Do you really know
anyone who is more
interesting than
your own kids?

❖ 29 ❖

Do you know
anyone who needs
you more?

❖ 30 ❖

Your kids think you're
a great cook even if you
make barely edible pasta.

❖ 31 ❖

Watching *Barney*
with your three-
year-old daughter.

❖ 32 ❖

After she turns four,
never watching that
purple blowhard again.

❧ 33 ❧

You can admit to your daughters—and only to your daughters—that you kind of, well, in a way, like Britney Spears.

❧ 34 ❧

You can admit to your sons you root for the Cubs.

❖ 35 ❖

Even your
dumbest jokes
make your
toddler giggle.

❖ 36 ❖

You can give your
toddler a nickel
and she thinks
you're a big spender.

❧ 37 ❧

To get your kids
to respond, you
only have to repeat
yourself six times.

❧ 38 ❧

You didn't want
a social life
anyway, did you?

�֍ 39 ֍

Getting the royal treatment
on Father's Day . . . and milking
it for everything it's worth.

✖ 40 ֍

Eventually, your baby will
sleep through the night.
In the meantime, your puffy
eyes are quite attractive.

❧ 41 ❧

Shopping for new foods
that your baby will even
try is a huge challenge
("This pepperoni/asparagus
looks pretty good").

❧ 42 ❧

Hearing your sweet
little daughter say her
first word. Of course,
that first word is *no.*

❈ 43 ❈

Turning on
your kids to
Frank Sinatra.

❈ 44 ❈

Hearing your
toddler's big finish on
"New York, New York."

❖ 45 ❖

Knowing you're twice
as big as the little boy
who's making fun of your
daughter at school.

❖ 46 ❖

Knowing you're
bigger than his
yuppie father, too.

❖ 47 ❖

Making big money this year?
Looking pretty darn handsome
with those new hair plugs?
Don't worry, the "terrible twos"
will humble you.

❖ 48 ❖

Ergo, so will
the tantrums
at Toys "R" Us.

❧ 49 ❧

You get to teach your kids time-tested jokes like "Pete and Repeat are in a boat and Pete falls out. Who's left?"

❧ 50 ❧

"Pete and Repeat are in a boat . . ."

❈ 51 ❈

Eventually,
your children go to
bed and you can get
your nightly ESPN fix.

❈ 52 ❈

As a father,
you get to revisit
Charlie Brown.

❧ 53 ❧

As a father, you
get to hear the sound
of "goo-goo."

❧ 54 ❧

As a father, you
get to sleep late . . .
when they turn twenty.

❧ 55 ❧

You get to experience the serene and peaceful world of Chuck E. Cheese.

❧ 56 ❧

You get to experience the charming, low-key world of soccer parents.

❧ 57 ❧

You may not be
able to compete
with Christmas, but
you can get your
kids hooked on
Jewish rye bread.

❧ 58 ❧

You feel like
Einstein after changing
your first diaper.

❧ 59 ❧

Your kids don't
ridicule you for the
hair in your ears.

❧ 60 ❧

They don't
ridicule you
because you
can't dunk.

❖ 61 ❖

But if they're still young enough, you can convince them you once dunked on Shaq.

❖ 62 ❖

Once your children turn five, you don't have to read to them while they're in the bathroom.

❖ 63 ❖

After you have a new baby, you are living proof that a man can function on four hours' sleep . . . kind of.

❖ 64 ❖

After you have a new baby, you want more!

❖ 65 ❖

On days when your kids are out of control, you dream about writing books called *Five Great Things About Being a Dad.*

❖ 66 ❖

Your kids are amazingly cute when they're not beating each other up.

❧ 67 ❧

It always makes you laugh
when your kids aren't in the
car and you realize you're
still listening to Weird Al.

❧ 68 ❧

How perfect do
your kids look while
they're sleeping?

❖ 69 ❖

How soft and warm
are they when
they wake up?

❖ 70 ❖

Once your kids
start playing soccer,
you can try out those
lovely Porta Potties.

The Simple Pleasures of Being a Dad

❧ 71 ❧

Watching your kid
become a star
at jump rope.

❧ 72 ❧

The beautiful
sound of your
baby's laughter.

❖ 73 ❖

The smell of
your children's hair
after their baths.

❖ 74 ❖

Getting called
"Daddy" all day.

❖ 75 ❖

Watching cartoons
with your kids on
Sunday morning.

❖ 76 ❖

Screaming,
"Yahtzee!"

❖ 77 ❖

Walking your kid
to school while
holding her hand.

❖ 78 ❖

Giving piggyback rides
and tying pigtails.

❖ 79 ❖

When your three-year-old
says, "I love you, Daddy,"
after climbing off the pony
at her birthday party.

❖ 80 ❖

Watching a sunset
with your children.

❖ 81 ❖

Whenever your kid
draws a fish,
it's always smiling.

❖ 82 ❖

Seeing them finally
ride their bikes down
the sidewalk without
you holding their seats.

❖ 83 ❖

Watching your child
onstage in her
first school play.

❖ 84 ❖

Watching her
at her first
ballet recital.

❖ 85 ❖

Those rare but precious
moments when your
kids get along and
help each other.

❖ 86 ❖

Popsicles!

❧ 87 ❧

When Mommy says,
"Yeah, right," you can
bribe your kids into
giving you back rubs.

❧ 88 ❧

Toddlers are
even cuter when
they're pouting.

❧ 89 ❧

Spending your
entire paycheck
on Beanie Babies.

❧ 90 ❧

You can train
your kids to
screen your calls.

❧ 91 ❧

The joy your
parents get from
having grandkids.

❧ 92 ❧

Kids make the
grocery store a
lot more fun.

❈ 93 ❈

They think it's
hysterical that
you're forty-two.

❈ 94 ❈

They think it's
hysterical when
Mommy points out
the shaving cream
in your ear.

❖ 95 ❖

You don't have
to leave the house
to be disrespected.

❖ 96 ❖

No matter how hard
they play, your children
never smell bad.

❧ 97 ❧

When you have a newborn baby, you have an excuse to drink espresso.

❧ 98 ❧

When you have a newborn baby, you're fine with that drool you're wearing.

❖ 99 ❖

Listening to
Radio Disney 24/7.

❖ 100 ❖

Listening to them
chat with their
grandparents
on the phone.

❖ 101 ❖

When your prayers
get answered . . . and
they turn out like
their mother.

❖ 102 ❖

It's fun to step on
sharp toys when you
get up at three A.M.
to calm the baby.

❖ 103 ❖

Unlike your disgusted wife, your kids will rub aloe on you when you're peeling.

❖ 104 ❖

You get to care for their goldfish, Mojo Jojo, when your kids get bored with him after three days.

❧ 105 ❧

Turning your kids on
to *Rocky and Bullwinkle*
(the classic TV show and
not the lame new movie).

❧ 106 ❧

Even your toddler's
bad breath smells
kind of sweet.

❖ 107 ❖

The surge of pride when
your kid learns how
to change channels
with the remote.

❖ 108 ❖

The sheer delight your
three-year-old derives
from mussing your hair.

❧ 109 ❧

Your three-year-old
only breaks twenty
or thirty of your
Itty Bitty booklights.

❧ 110 ❧

Your children
don't care what your
bowling score was.

✤ 111 ✤

Knowing what they will say before they say it.

✤ 112 ✤

You get to ponder life's big questions: Why do 1,250 Chuck E. Cheese game tickets only equal a $1.25 toy?

❖ 113 ❖

You get to spend hours
each day trying to
locate your baby's
favorite pink bottle.

❖ 114 ❖

Your children come through
like champs when you and
your wife finally leave
town without them.

❧ 115 ❧

Hearing your
daughter's friend say,
"I like your dad."

❧ 116 ❧

Not hearing your
daughter's friend say,
"You got a light?"

❧ 117 ❧

Hearing your daughter's
friend say, "I'll see
you at Girl Scouts."

❧ 118 ❧

Not hearing your
daughter's friend say,
"I'll hook up with you
at the Eminem concert."

❖ 61 ❖

❖ 119 ❖

When your wife goes
on business trips, you
get all the good-night
hugs and kisses.

❖ 120 ❖

When your wife goes
on business trips, you
develop profound respect
for single parents.

❧ 121 ❧

How cute does
your toddler look
in a French braid?

❧ 122 ❧

When your children
clean their bedrooms
without being
threatened or bribed.

❈ 123 ❈

Your wife and kids
still talk about that day
at the petting zoo when
you told a pushy llama
to "back off."

❈ 124 ❈

You stop feeling like
an ogre when you tell your
child her time-out is over.

❧ 125 ❧

You can sing
the lyrics to *Annie*
in your sleep.

❧ 126 ❧

You can make your
toddler happy by letting
her push the elevator button.

❖ 127 ❖

You feel like a big man
when you let them
stay up an hour later.

❖ 128 ❖

Christmas is far
more fun when
kids are involved.

❖ 129 ❖

Having smart kids
confuses your enemies.

❖ 130 ❖

Having smart kids
makes you think,
"Maybe I'm not such
a pinhead after all."

❧ 131 ❧

Seeing your kid's excitement,
not at losing that first tooth,
but at pocketing that seven
bucks from the tooth fairy.

❧ 132 ❧

Hearing your kids
use your dad's
favorite wisecracks.

❧ 133 ❧

You may not be wealthy, or even wise, but your wife loves you because you're a good daddy.

❧ 134 ❧

Your kids will get you snacks when you're too lazy to move an inch off the couch.

❧ 135 ❧

You can astonish
them with your
ability to make eggs.

❧ 136 ❧

You have an excuse to
stop acting macho (which
nobody bought anyway)
and just be yourself.

❧ 137 ❧

Your children
keep you
(relatively)
young.

❧ 138 ❧

You can buy just
about any birthday
card because your kid
won't read it anyway.

❖ 139 ❖

Your parents
visit more because
you have kids.

❖ 140 ❖

Your in-laws
visit less because
you have kids.

❖ 141 ❖

Your toddler
thinks your earlobes
are funny.

❖ 142 ❖

Your toddler
thinks life
itself is funny.

❧ 143 ❧

You can work
at home and spend
time with your toddler.

❧ 144 ❧

You can lock your office
door when you hear your
toddler freaking out.

❖ 145 ❖

You stop wondering
if your life will
ever have meaning.

❖ 146 ❖

No one can
force you to buy
Harry Potter books.

❈ 147 ❖

Knowing your kids
have their grandfather's
sense of humor.

❈ 148 ❖

Knowing they have
their grandmother's
kindness.

❧ 149 ❧

Knowing your kids are
awesome mostly because
they have an awesome mother.

❧ 150 ❧

Watching your wife and kids
play at the park . . . and
knowing you truly are blessed.

❈ 151 ❈

Okay, so your toddler
snapped on her first vacation.
Then again, it was also
her last vacation.

❈ 152 ❈

Videos of your kids are
better than 90 percent
of Hollywood movies.

❧ 153 ❧

Videos of your kids
can drive unwanted
people from your home.

❧ 154 ❧

Unlike their mother,
your kids don't think you're
a jerk when you get lost
driving home from places
you've been to before.

❧ 155 ❧

Sea World.
The San Diego Zoo.
Disneyland.

❧ 156 ❧

The desert.
The ocean.
The mountains.

❖ 157 ❖

Unlike you,
your kids don't
still draw stick people.

❖ 158 ❖

How cute
are baby
gym shoes?

Lessons You Learn from Fatherhood

❖ 159 ❖

What a huge
racket children's
furniture is.

❖ 160 ❖

To be your
kids' mentor and
not their boss.

❧ 161 ❧

To really listen
when they talk.

❧ 162 ❧

To treat them
as well as you treat
your best friends.

❧ 163 ❧

That you may be lacking
in many ways, but
being a good father
makes up for a lot.

❧ 164 ❧

Returning from a
business trip and knowing
you're exactly where
you want to be.

❖ 165 ❖

Being a dad makes you
less self-absorbed, which is
also a good development
for your wife.

❖ 166 ❖

Once you see you're
not a perfect father,
it's much easier to
forgive your own dad.

❧ 167 ❧

You can avoid your father's mistakes and build on his strengths.

❧ 168 ❧

You find that admitting your own mistakes is very healthy.

❖ 169 ❖

Seeing your child's
homework and realizing
she is smarter than you.

❖ 170 ❖

And yet, realizing,
in a pinch, you
can still do math.

❖ 171 ❖

After you've had
a few kids, not every
bump and bruise
becomes a crisis.

❖ 172 ❖

Playing "Go Fish"
is very, very relaxing.

❧ 173 ❧

Your best friends
are fathers, too.

❧ 174 ❧

Your best friends
understand when you
cancel because your
kid is sick.

❧ 175 ❧

Your best friends
don't tell your kids
what a maniac
you used to be.

❧ 176 ❧

Without any help from
your wife, you dress your
kid in the morning and
her clothes match!

❖ 177 ❖

You have always wanted a Suburban and now you have enough offspring to need one.

❖ 178 ❖

If you have an aunt with a beard, you can tell your kids she's on your wife's side.

❖ 179 ❖

You look almost frightening
in the morning, but your
kids roll out of bed
with perfect hair.

❖ 180 ❖

Being a dad
is better than
being a kiwi.

❈ 181 ❈

Your children's
friends are loyal,
sweet, and darling.

❈ 182 ❈

Your children's
friends eventually
go home.

❖ 183 ❖

Going to the
video store makes
your kids gleeful.

❖ 184 ❖

Finding a good
public school.

❖ 185 ❖

Soon they'll be
old enough to watch
Caddyshack with you.

❖ 186 ❖

Soon they'll be
old enough to
"get" Bill Murray.

❧ 187 ❧

Knowing you have
a nanny who loves
your children.

❧ 188 ❧

Knowing she loved
them even before they
were potty trained.

❧ 189 ❧

You can talk baseball with your pediatrician. In fact, he loves baseball so deeply that you can hear other kids crying down the hall while he is fondly recalling the 1951 Cleveland Indians.

❧ 190 ❧

When you hear a doctor is all business . . . and he turns into a softy around your kid.

❧ 191 ❧

Knowing your child's
teacher likes your kid.
And cares about your kid.
And is going to miss your
kid when she moves on.

❧ 192 ❧

Your kids like being
tickled, but they don't
insist on tickling you.

❖ 193 ❖

Toddlers are
flat-out funny.

❖ 194 ❖

Even if your wife is
from California, you can
still teach your kids to
use Chicago expressions
like "flat-out."

❧ 195 ❧

Knowing your kids have
your Chicago persistence
and your wife's
California optimism.

❧ 196 ❧

Being flexible enough
to accept it when your
kids say they want to
move to New York.

❈ 197 ❈

Being rigid enough
to nix it when they say
they want to move to Utah.

❈ 198 ❈

Even if you don't know
any lullabies yet, you can
sing them Springsteen
when they're babies.

❧ 199 ❧

You can introduce
your kids to Motown
and maybe they'll have
soul even if they're white.

❧ 200 ❧

You can convince
your kids that any music
at all is basically cool
(except for mean-spirited rap).

❧ 201 ❧

Whenever your kid
draws a cow, it's always
wearing a bell around its neck.

❧ 202 ❧

Your kids are always
ecstatic at the beach
(and you're a happy
guy, too).

❧ 203 ❧

Watching your children
frolic in the surf
(a couple feet away
from Miss California).

❧ 204 ❧

If your children like you,
who cares about that tyrant
called your boss?

❖ 205 ❖

Having kids to support
keeps you from telling
your boss what you
really think.

❖ 206 ❖

Calling diapers
"dipeys" like they
do on *Rugrats.*

❧ 207 ❧

You can raid
your kid's piggy bank
when you're broke.

❧ 208 ❧

How cute does your kid
look wearing your T-shirt
down to her knees?

❧ 209 ❧

When your kid learns
to count and can finally
handle the bank in Monopoly.

❧ 210 ❧

You can position the
Monopoly board so you
can still catch glimpses
of the World Series.

❧ 211 ❧

Babies
still take naps!

❧ 212 ❧

When everything else fails,
the noise from a vacuum
cleaner really does put
most babies to sleep.

❖ 213 ❖

For two years you've unplugged the phone, tiptoed around the house, and done everything else in your power to make sure your napping baby doesn't wake up. Then one day you get a new roof and your baby sleeps right through it. How liberated you feel . . . and how idiotic.

❖ 214 ❖

Potty jokes
never fail when
your kids are crying.

❖ 215 ❖

Neither does
the "pull my
finger" trick.

❧ 216 ❧

Having kids who
see right through you
keeps you from being
even phonier than
you are now.

❧ 217 ❧

Your children's obsession
with *Gilligan's Island*
will pass.

❖ 218 ❖

Watching *The Brady Bunch*
makes your own family
seem normal.

❖ 219 ❖

Anything new to you is
paralyzing, but anything new
to your children is exciting.

❧ 220 ❧

When your toddler
enters the room wearing
your high-tops.

❧ 221 ❧

Your toddler gets
pumped up when you
take her with you
to get the mail.

❖ 222 ❖

Sometimes your
five-year-old still lets
you kiss her before she
runs into kindergarten.

❖ 223 ❖

Volunteering in
kindergarten
reduces stress.

❧ 224 ❧

Seeing other dads
with kids who are
more out-of-control
than yours are.

❧ 225 ❧

Seeing other dads
with bigger guts
than yours.

❧ 226 ❧

When you're trying to
parallel park, it's important
to get advice from those
who don't drive yet.

❧ 227 ❧

It gives you a good
laugh when their
overfed goldfish starts
to resemble Shamu.

❧ 228 ❧

They think you're
really tough when
you catch spiders.

❧ 229 ❧

They think you're
really sensitive when
you don't kill them.

❖ 230 ❖

How cute
do your kids look
after a haircut?

❖ 231 ❖

You can look in
their rooms when
they're sleeping
and see angels.

❧ 232 ☙

You have the power
to veto children's
TV shows you
don't like.

❧ 233 ☙

Watching your kid
discover the joy
of bonbons.

❧ 234 ❧

Watching your kids
eat every last sprinkle
off their ice cream.

❧ 235 ❧

Your kids believe it
when you swear they
need sunblock.

❖ 236 ❖

When you're stressing about work and your toddler walks in wearing nothing but Mommy's high heels.

❖ 237 ❖

They look at you like you're Gandhi when you let them eat dinner in the den.

❧ 238 ❧

If they go ballistic on airplanes, you can usually calm them down by suggesting they cover their seat belts with stickers.

❧ 239 ❧

Seeing your five-year-old in her Brownie uniform for the first time.

❧ 240 ❧

Your toddler is
not self-conscious
about her tummy.

❧ 241 ❧

Taking your kids on
walks and remembering
how lovely nature is.

❖ 242 ❖

Taking along a baby
makes any errand at
all more entertaining.

❖ 243 ❖

Holding a sleeping baby
through an entire *Monday
Night Football* game.

❧ 244 ❧

When your baby
finally wakes up
and you can stretch.

❧ 245 ❧

Sesame Street.

Great Things

About

Being a Kid

with

Your Kids

❧ 246 ❧

You can mooch
their Snickers
on Halloween.

❧ 247 ❧

When you take them
to the zoo, they know
more about the animals
than you do.

❧ 248 ❧

Playing hooky
from work and
taking them to
the ballpark.

❧ 249 ❧

Climbing on the
monkey bars
with them.

❧ 250 ❧

You get
to play with
their coolest toys.

❧ 251 ❧

You get to reread
White Fang and
Call of the Wild.

❖ 252 ❖

You have an
excuse to watch
The Wizard of Oz.

❖ 253 ❖

You have an
excuse to say the
word *Pikachu.*

❖ 254 ❖

Reading your
children anything
written by
Shel Silverstein,
but especially
The Giving Tree.

❖ 255 ❖

Dr. Seuss!

❧ 256 ❧

It's amusing at the gym when you open your shaving kit and discover you've brought *Sesame Street* toothpaste.

❧ 257 ❧

When you have your third daughter and your best friend calls up and asks for *Petticoat Junction*.

❧ 258 ❧

Reading to your kid's class
and scaring them silly by
yelling the word *BOO!*
in a Halloween story.

❧ 259 ❧

Reading to your kid's class
and seeing she is happy
that you're there.

❧ 260 ❧

Your kids think
your muscles are
bigger than Arnold's.

❧ 261 ❧

Pushing that
double stroller is
good for the pecs.

❖ 262 ❖

Your kids
(unlike your wife)
don't care if you leave
the toilet seat up.

❖ 263 ❖

When your children get
hooked on *Powerpuff Girls*
and start referring to
you as Mojo Jojo.

❧ 264 ❧

Watching your children
have a great time
with their cousins.

❧ 265 ❧

When you take your three-year-
old to see the play *Beauty and the
Beast* . . . and she bursts into tears
the first time the Beast screams at
Belle . . . but then hangs tough
and has the time of her life.

❖ 266 ❖

Having daughters
who insist on putting
up Spice Girls posters.

❖ 267 ❖

Come on, admit it.
You like it when
your kids fight
for your attention.

❧ 268 ❧

Parents' night at school—
when they neatly arrange
their desk so you can
review their work.

❧ 269 ❧

When the parent-teacher
conference is all good news.

❖ 270 ❖

The pleasure your kids get
when you wear that loud
orange shirt they bought
for your birthday.

❖ 271 ❖

It's an intellectual challenge
trying to fend off their reasons
for staying up late.

❖ 272 ❖

You always have
a good reason
to go home.

❖ 273 ❖

Knowing that if you
get hit by a cement truck,
your kids will still have the
best mommy in the world.

❖ 274 ❖

Waking up at three A.M. to find out your child is using you as a pillow.

❖ 275 ❖

The first day of school is exciting for the whole family.

❖ 276 ❖

Sneaking out of their
bedrooms without waking
them up . . . and knowing the
remote control is all yours.

❖ 277 ❖

Saying,
"Just two more bites,"
and they take three.

❖ 278 ❖

Your kids think it's funny
when instead of saying
"vomit," you say "yammy."

❖ 279 ❖

If you're stuck at a
boring party, you can
lie about having to
get the sitter home.

❖ 280 ❖

Those historic occasions
when your children go
to bed without a fight.

❖ 281 ❖

Unashamedly
calling your toddler's
teacher Miss Barbara.

❧ 282 ❧

Writing stories with your kids about a big red bouncing ball named Benny.

❧ 283 ❧

How cute is it when they set up a lemonade stand?

❧ 284 ❧

How cute is it
when they help
you wash the car?

❧ 285 ❧

When your own parents
are feeling blue, they get
cheered up by watching
videos of your kids.

❖ 286 ❖

You feel
truly thankful
on Thanksgiving.

❖ 287 ❖

You feel
truly thankful
every day.

❧ 288 ❧

Once every few years, by
some freak of nature, you
meet someone without
children and you have
a whole conversation
without saying "poop."

❧ 289 ❧

How adorable is your
toddler when she runs?

❖ 290 ❖

You may not be
as smooth as your wife,
but you're still respectable
at changing diapers.

❖ 291 ❖

Eventually,
your toddler
will stop biting.

❖ 292 ❖

You can teach
your kids not to
tattle on each other.

❖ 293 ❖

But they'll do it anyway.
So at least you'll know
what's going on.

❧ 294 ❧

They're not embarrassed
to be with you when
they're still little.

❧ 295 ❧

When you mildly criticize
one of their friends and
they respond with
ferocious loyalty.

❖ 296 ❖

If you let them mess up
your hair at home, they'll
usually agree not to
do it in public.

❖ 297 ❖

Hearing your toddler create
new pronunciations
("My favorite color is ocean"—
when she means orange.)

❖ 298 ❖

Your toddler doesn't *always* wet her bed.

❖ 299 ❖

Watching your toddler, who used to be scared of the water, swimming the length of the pool after her lessons.

❧ 300 ❧

It brings back memories
when they make homemade
forts with blankets and chairs.

❧ 301 ❧

When you fight with your wife,
having children increases the
odds of making up quickly.

❧ 302 ❧

Since you're an afterthought
when your wife makes home
videos, you can lie on the
couch like a beached whale
while your children ham
it up like Jerry Lewis.

❧ 303 ❧

Being a father makes
you feel less shallow.

❧ 304 ❧

You're more patient
when babies go
"WWAAAAHHH"
on airplanes.

❧ 305 ❧

Toddlers are easy to tackle
when they won't stay still
for a diaper change.

❧ 306 ❧

You can ignore the latest trends and name your daughters Emma, Grace, and Hannah.

❧ 307 ❧

Once you name your kids, you can throw out those inane books about naming kids ("Joshua meant 'pool boy' in ancient Greece").

❧ 308 ❧

You're a working stiff
and a family man.
So you have an
excuse not to be tan.

❧ 309 ❧

Watching your wife
give birth and
thanking God.

❖ 310 ❖

When your
new baby really
does resemble you.

❖ 311 ❖

But not as much
as she resembles
her pretty mommy.

❧ 312 ❧

When you carry her into the
house for the first time . . .
a moment you'll never
forget the rest of your life.

❧ 313 ❧

Stocking the
changing table
is an art form.

❈ 314 ❈

The first time
she hugs you
around the neck.

❈ 315 ❈

The first time
she smiles . . . and not
because she's passed gas.

❧ 316 ❧

No matter how dazed
and confused you are, there's
always a new dad who's even
more clueless than you.

❧ 317 ❧

You can spend countless
hours debating the cry-it-out
method with other parents.

❖ 318 ❖

Playing peekaboo
can amuse a
baby for hours.

❖ 319 ❖

Playing peekaboo
reminds you
to lighten up!

❖ 320 ❖

Having a crib
in the house is
good for your soul.

❖ 321 ❖

Kissing your toddler's
tummy and hearing
her squeal with delight.

❧ 322 ❧

Sure, you hate leaving town on business trips, but you also love getting a full night's sleep.

❧ 323 ❧

Coming up with ridiculous nicknames for your toddler—Pinky Santa Claus Big Diaper Head, for example.

❧ 324 ❧

You become an expert at distraction ("I understand you want your sister's toy, but have you ever noticed that Yogi Bear walks around naked except for his hat and tie?").

❧ 325 ❧

The first time your toddler goes on the potty!

❧ 326 ❧

The people at work always gush over how cute your kids look in their pictures.

❧ 327 ❧

To you, the pictures *are* incredibly cute . . . even if your coworkers are lying.

❧ 328 ❧

Even though you once
swore you'd never use videos
as a baby-sitter, you can pop
one in and get stuff done.

❧ 329 ❧

Having kids is
a lifelong excuse
for running late.

Watching as Your Children Get Older

❖ 330 ❖

Seeing them go
from toddlers to
"little kids."

❖ 331 ❖

Seeing them
grow up with
decent values.

❖ 332 ❖

Seeing their
self-esteem grow,
but not their ego.

❖ 333 ❖

Seeing them
conquer one
of their fears.

❧ 334 ❧

When your kids
actually take no
for an answer.

❧ 335 ❧

Seeing your six-year-old
daughter kiss a boy
on the cheek . . . and
your intense relief
when he runs away.

❧ 336 ❧

When your daughters
are old enough to
date . . . well . . .
maybe not.

❧ 337 ❧

Watching them
get their high
school diploma.

❧ 338 ❧

Saving for their
college education.

❧ 339 ❧

Having them
support you when
you're feeble.

❊ 340 ❊

Seeing your baby laugh
hysterically the first time
she's old enough to realize
your family has a dog.

❊ 341 ❊

Seeing her not fall off
when she tries riding your
dog like he's a horse.

❧ 342 ❧

Seeing your faithful
dog sleep under
your baby's crib.

❧ 343 ❧

Accepting the cold hard truth:
The dog loves the baby because
she keeps dropping food.

❧ 344 ❧

Loving someone enough to put on a woman's hat and jump around like a pansy in order to give her a "funny show" before her bedtime.

❧ 345 ❧

Those baseball cards with your kid's picture on them ("Lester likes to fingerpaint in the off-season").

❖ 346 ❖

Meeting Mary-Kate and Ashley,
the Olsen twins, and having your
children think you're a god.

❖ 347 ❖

If their bedtime story stars
them ... and if they're saving
animals in danger ... your
children go to sleep happy.

❖ 348 ❖

Seeing one of
your good traits
in your children.

❖ 349 ❖

Seeing one of
your lousy traits
in the kid next door.

❧ 350 ❧

When you start to sound
like your dad . . . and
it's not a bad thing.

❧ 351 ❧

GapKids has
the hippest
clothes on earth.

❧ 352 ❧

The goose-bumpy feeling
you get when your kid
takes her first steps.

❧ 353 ❧

The tears in your eyes
when she first
calls you Da-da.

❧ 354 ❧

The tears in your eyes
when her college
tuition bill arrives.

❧ 355 ❧

When you finally take a
vacation without your children,
how incredibly grateful you
are to be alone with your
wife in a hotel room.

❧ 356 ❧

When it comes to fathers and daughters, it feels good to be wrapped around their fingers.

❧ 357 ❧

Being blindfolded on Father's Day, guided into the car, and driven to the bowling alley.

❧ 358 ❧

Dancing your
baby asleep to
Natalie Merchant.

❧ 359 ❧

Cuddling with your wife
the minute you know the
baby's really snoozing.

❧ 360 ❧

You enjoy grocery shopping because even the smallest things you do for your family feel good.

❧ 361 ❧

You get to wimp out of going to bachelor parties.

❧ 362 ❧

When your kids
do the right thing
without being told.

❧ 363 ❧

When your toddler
pushes you out of the
bathroom, closes the
door, and says,
"I want privacy, Daddy."

❧ 364 ❧

Spending
New Year's Eve
at home with
your children.

❧ 365 ❧

Telling your kids
the story of how you
met and fell in love
with their mommy.

❧ 366 ❧

Hearing other
people compliment
your child.

❧ 367 ❧

Knowing your
kids are far more
creative than you.

❧ 368 ❧

Knowing your kids
are nice to your
elderly neighbors.

❧ 369 ❧

How excited your
kids get when you
set up play dates.

❈ 370 ❈

Listening to
your kid wish
on a star.

❈ 371 ❈

Entirely work-free
weekends spent
with your kid.

❧ 372 ❧

Whispering to your
child while she is
still inside her
mommy's womb.

❧ 373 ❧

Hearing your child
be truthful when
she breaks something.

❈ 374 ❈

Seeing your child
make friends with
a child a different
color than her own.

❈ 375 ❈

Accepting that your kids
will never be perfect . . .
and even loving their flaws.

❧ 376 ❧

Having your children
forgive you when
you screw up.

❧ 377 ❧

Easter egg hunts
are comical with
small children.

❈ 378 ❧

How cute are small children doing karate?

❈ 379 ❧

Writing your children poems on every birthday.

❖ 380 ❖

Strolling with
your kids on
warm rainy days.

❖ 381 ❖

Watching your
kid devour her
first brownie.

❧ 382 ❧

The miraculous
moment your
baby is born.

❧ 383 ❧

When you walk by your
five-year-old's room and
she's reading *The Cat in
the Hat* all by herself.

❧ 384 ❧

When, thank God,
your children eat
their veggies.

❧ 385 ❧

Reading *Winnie-the-Pooh* to
your preschooler, *The Berenstain
Bears* to your kindergartner,
and The Magic Tree House
series to your second grader.

❖ 386 ❖

Coming to your kids'
rescue when they scream,
"Dad, I need some toilet paper!"

❖ 387 ❖

Your kids don't
panic when they
have to visit the dentist.

❧ 388 ❧

Your kids like the toys at Burger King, but they can do without eating the food.

❧ 389 ❧

Teasing your seven-year-old about the boys she likes at school.

❧ 390 ❧

Remembering
the charm of
Valentine's Day.

❧ 391 ❧

Dancing with
your daughter
at a wedding.

❖ 392 ❖

When sibling rivalry is making the whole house crazy, you can whisk them off to Toys "R" Us.

❖ 393 ❖

When other parents say how easy it was watching your kids.

❧ 394 ❧

When your
kids show
their manners.

❧ 395 ❧

When they
show they know
right from wrong.

❧ 396 ❧

The pure joy
of seeing
them improve.

❧ 397 ❧

Knowing that being a
daddy is so much easier
than being a mommy.

❧ 398 ❧

If you're on a tight
deadline, knowing
that Mommy can
handle them herself.

❧ 399 ❧

Having someone to
explain how to work
the computer.

❖ 400 ❖

Seeing your kid's surprise
when she walks out of class
and finds you waiting.

❖ 401 ❖

Then taking your
kid to lunch—
just the two of you.

❧ 402 ❧

Their excitement
when they see
Santa Claus's
presents.

❧ 403 ❧

Their first dive
into the pool!

❖ 404 ❖

Their first night
without a wet bed.

❖ 405 ❖

Their delight
after finishing their
first snowman.

❖ 406 ❖

The thrill they get
from catching
their first fish.

❖ 407 ❖

Coming home
to them after a
bad day at work.

❖ 408 ❖

The unconditional
trust they have
in you.

❖ 409 ❖

They love you
simply because
you're their daddy.

❖ 410 ❖

The unexpected things
that toddlers say
("Dad, I'm going to call
you Poo-Poo Head").

❖ 411 ❖

Hearing them say,
"I love you," just
before they fall asleep.

❧ 412 ❧

The comical sight
of your toddler
flossing her teeth.

❧ 413 ❧

Receiving a homemade
gift your children
worked hard on.

The Best

Things

About

Kids and

Sports

❈ 414 ❈

Taking them to
the gym where
you work out.

❈ 415 ❈

Naming them after
your favorite sports stars
("It's time for bed, Piazza!").

❖ 416 ❖

Playing tag with them
and showing off
your amazingly
athletic moves.

❖ 417 ❖

Teaching your
daughters to
love basketball.

❧ 418 ❧

Brainwashing them into being Chicago Bulls fans (though this has become more difficult post-Jordan).

❧ 419 ❧

Shooting baskets with them in the driveway.

❖ 420 ❖

The glorious day
when they make
their first shot.

❖ 421 ❖

The not quite as glorious,
but nonetheless fulfilling
day when they get their
first offensive rebound.

❧ 422 ❧

Taking along your kids means you can leave boring baseball games in the fifth inning.

❧ 423 ❧

For those of us who loathe golf, spending time with our kids gives us a perfect reason never to learn.

❖ 424 ❖

Rather than watching
pro football on Sundays,
you get to chauffeur your kids
to their own sporting events.

❖ 425 ❖

The proud looks on their
faces when you hit a home run
at the company picnic.

❈ 426 ❈

It's perfectly okay if your
kids are not as athletic
as you are. You're not
as intelligent as they are.

❈ 427 ❈

Coaching your child
in any sport . . .
even soccer.

❈ 428 ❈

Eventually, the soccer
season will end.

❈ 429 ❈

When your kids accept
that winning in sports isn't
everything, and that what
really matters the most
is a good sweat.

❈ 430 ❈

Seeing them walk in
with their report
card—smiling.

❈ 431 ❈

On vacation, the first few
minutes in the hotel room—
watching them investigate
everything from the mini-
fridge to the shampoos.

❧ 432 ❧

Lying in bed with your
child . . . telling stories . . .
listening to her questions
about life . . . the quiet moments.

❧ 433 ❧

The proud look on her face
when Daddy wins her
a prize at the carnival.

❧ 434 ❧

If you don't know
the answers to your kid's
questions, you can
always find an
expert who does.

❧ 435 ❧

FAO Schwartz!

❖ 436 ❖

Loving someone enough
to dress up as Big Bird
on her birthday.

❖ 437 ❖

When your children
inherit your own
love of books.

❖ 438 ❖

Letting your
kids take baths
by candlelight.

❖ 439 ❖

Going outside
at night and
watching the stars.

❖ 440 ❖

Sitting by the
window and
watching the
lightning.

❖ 441 ❖

Spotting a rainbow
together after it rains.

❖ 442 ❖

Teaching your kids
the science behind the
lightning and rainbows.

❖ 443 ❖

Skateboarding with your
child—as long as no one
winds up in the ER.

❖ 444 ❖

When you enter the
room and your child
says, "I love you,"
in sign language.

❖ 445 ❖

Staring at your children's
pictures before diving into
another day of work.

❖ 446 ❖

When your kid
volunteers to write
a thank-you note.

❖ 447 ❖

When she
volunteers to clean
up her own mess.

❖ 448 ❖

Eating popcorn and sipping
hot chocolate in front of
the fireplace with them.

❖ 449 ❖

Having a picnic with them
and never having a single
thought about work.

❈ 450 ❈

Putting your children's
needs in front of your own
makes you feel good.

❈ 451 ❈

No matter how cranky
your toddler gets, she'll
cheer up if you let her play
with pots and pans.

❈ 452 ❈

Your kids think you're
a great man if you let
them buy treats from
the ice-cream truck.

❈ 453 ❈

Toddlers shine like
the sun when they
eat cotton candy.

❧ 454 ❧

When you move
into a new home and
your kids bravely say they
like it more than the old one.

❧ 455 ❧

When she walks in the door
smiling because she made a
friend at her new school.

❧ 456 ❧

When you finally realize
that your kids are far too
sharp for child psychology.

❧ 457 ❧

When your previously
shy kid starts telling intricate
stories on the playground.

❧ 458 ❧

Giving your toddler
nose-to-nose
"Eskimo kisses."

❧ 459 ❧

Seeing your toddler learn
how to drive her Barbie jeep
without doing a number on
the neighbor's mailbox.

❖ 460 ❖

How cute does
your toddler look
in her sunglasses?

❖ 461 ❖

The awe in your
children's eyes
when they see the
Grand Canyon.

❖ 462 ❖

How early
they pass out
after hiking all day!

❖ 463 ❖

Saying,
"You're a great kid,"
and meaning it.

❖ 464 ❖

If her throat is sore enough,
you can turn her on
to chamomile tea.

❖ 465 ❖

If they're hungry
enough, they'll eat
nutritious food.

❧ 466 ❧

If they're tired enough, they'll fall asleep in the car on the way home.

❧ 467 ❧

New babies make you stop sweating the small stuff.

❖ 468 ❖

New babies give
you a reason to read
Paul Reiser's great
book *Babyhood.*

❖ 469 ❖

Giving your kid
your old high school
football jersey.

❖ 470 ❖

Giving your kid
a tour of where
you work.

❖ 471 ❖

Giving your kids
plenty of attention, but
also knowing when they
need their space.

❈ 472 ❈

Your kids think it's
an adventure when
you take them to
the public library.

❈ 473 ❈

They burst with pride
when they get their
library cards.

❧ 474 ❧

Then they mix up the library
books with their own books,
and you have to pay the late fees.
But, on the other hand, the library
needs the money. And so in a way
they've helped the community.

❧ 475 ❧

Being a father teaches you
to look on the bright side.

❖ 476 ❖

How relaxing
are tea parties
with toddlers?

❖ 477 ❖

When your children
show an interest in
hearing about the lives
of their grandparents.

❈ 478 ❈

When your sometimes obnoxious
children turn into model kids
around their grandparents.

❈ 479 ❈

By allowing your kids to
have a slumber party, you
can demand good behavior
the whole week before.